BRITAIN IN OLD PHOTOGRAPHS

KINVER &
ENVILLE

BOB CLARKE & TONY FREER

SUTTON PUBLISHING LIMITED

Sutton Publishing Limited
Phoenix Mill · Far Thrupp · Stroud
Gloucestershire · GL5 2BU

First published 1996

Cover photographs: *front*: the White Harte
Hotel, *c.* 1906; *back*: a motoring party visits
'The Cherry Tree', *c.* 1918.

British Library Cataloguing in Publication Data
A catalogue record for this book is available from the
British Library.

ISBN 0-7509-1293-6

Typeset in 10/12 Perpetua.
Typesetting and origination by
Sutton Publishing Limited.
Printed in Great Britain by
Ebenezer Baylis, Worcester.

THE BLACK COUNTRY SOCIETY

This voluntary society, affiliated to the Civic Trust, was founded in 1967 as a reaction to
the trend of the late 1950s and early 1960s to amalgamate everything into large units and
in the Midlands to sweep away the area's industrial heritage in the process.

The general aim of the Society is to create interest in the past, present and future of
the Black Country, and early on, it campaigned for the establishment of an industrial
museum. In 1975 the Black Country Museum was started by Dudley Borough Council
on 26 acres of totally derelict land adjoining the grounds of Dudley Castle. This has
developed into an award-winning museum which attracts over 250,000 visitors annually.

There are over two thousand members of the Black Country Society and all receive
the quarterly magazine *The Blackcountryman*, of which over 112 issues have been
published since its founding in 1967. In the whole collection there are some 1,700
authoritative articles on all aspects of the Black Country by historians, teachers,
researchers, students, subject experts and ordinary folk with an extraordinary story to tell.
The whole constitutes a unique resource about the area and is a mine of information for
students and researchers who frequently refer to it. Many schools and libraries are
subscribers. Three thousand copies of the magazine are printed each quarter. It is non-
commercial, and contributors do not receive payment for their articles.

PO Box 71 · Kingswinford · West Midlands DY6 9YN

CONTENTS

If you are **FED** with everything **UP** come to **KINVER**.

"THEO"

INTRODUCTION

Today's village of Kinver, in modern parlance a 'large' village of some 8,000 people, first made an appearance in 736 AD as 'Cynibre', the name relating to a woodland. In 964 the area was known as 'Cynfare' (a Royal road) and in the Domesday Book of 1086 as 'Chenevare' (a great ridge or edge), King's land and in which there were two mills and a manor.

Despite being close to what was to become the Black Country and, from the 17th century to the mid-19th century with a flourishing iron working industry powered by the River Stour, it still managed to avoid the spread of industry and housing. Instead it developed into a self-contained community which today maintains its individuality having successfully resisted the continuing expansion of the West Midland conurbation.

There is no doubt that in remaining an individual, if not a unique community, Kinver has been helped by its geographic location set amidst hilly countryside, separated from the encroaching suburbs by an arterial road, a river, a canal and, most importantly, surrounded by green belt land with much of the village being a designated conservation area.

From its origins as a Royal Hunting forest and being within one of the most scenically attractive areas in the Midlands, Kinver attracted many wealthy and influential landowners, several of whom were associated with the wool and, later, iron industries.

However, with the decline of the iron working industry in the 19th century, the village population fell as many families moved out to work in the flourishing industries of the Black Country or emigrated overseas.

Kinver as we know it today began to develop at the turn of the 20th century with the arrival of the Kinver Light Railway, offering a cheap and reliable transport system. Thus the first steps in the commuter age began and, at the same time, Kinver's unique rural attraction came within economic reach of tens of thousands of people who eagerly took the opportunity 'for a day out in the country'.

Although Kinver in some respects came to be regarded (and still is) as a dormitory area for Black Country industry and commerce, the village managed to retain its own identity and develop a thriving tourist industry. By the time the railway closed, Kinver had a regular bus service to Stourbridge and many coach operators were quick to capitalize on Kinver's attraction as a day and half-day excursion venue. With the arrival of the motor car, especially since 1950, Kinver has maintained its popularity. The great escarpment of Kinver Edge, the remains of its Iron Age fort earthworks and its National Trust heathland, the woods and rock houses all tower above the village to give it a special appeal to visitors and inhabitants alike.

In the following pages a century of the development of an unpretentious country village into a lively and diverse community, which still retains the essentials of English village life, is traced in words and photographs.

THE KINVER LIGHT RAILWAY

Opened in 1901, the Kinver Light Railway ran from the Fish Inn, Amblecote (Stourbridge) to Kinver, until 1930 when it fell victim to competition from road transport and closed.

More popularly known as 'the Kinver Trams', these vehicles carried thousands of day-trippers from the Black Country and Birmingham during their comparatively short life. By the time buses, cars and coaches made their appearance, Kinver had become a major venue for people escaping from the grime and smoke of the Black Country for a day out 'in the country'. Leaving Amblecote, the line travelled through Wollaston and along the Bridgnorth Road to the Stewponey and Foley Arms Hotel, Stourton. From there it crossed the Staffordshire and Worcestershire Canal and the River Stour to begin its journey through meadows and woodland to Kinver village.

A scene at the Stewponey & Foley Arms Hotel shortly after the tramway opened in 1901, where pedestrians, ponies and traps await the arrival (far left) of the tram from Amblecote to Kinver. The reference to 'Foley Arms' relates to the Foley family who, having made a vast fortune from the iron working industry in the Stour Valley and Black Country, became generous benefactors to many worthy causes in the area.

Changing times, c. 1920. The age of the motor car had arrived, a new licensee, Mr Berry, was mine host at the Stewponey, trees had begun to grow on the forecourt, the flagpole had disappeared and, although still operating, the line was carrying fewer passengers.

When the line closed in 1930, its bridge over the canal was demolished and a new road bridge carrying the A458 Bridgnorth Road was built on roughly the same site.

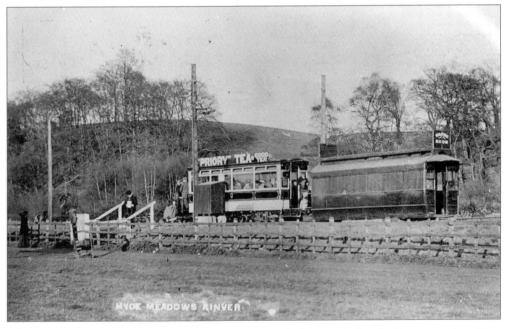

Next stop, Kinver . . . Hyde Meadows Halt, c. 1909, was the last stop before the Kinver terminus. Note the old tramcar body converted into a waiting room. Hyde Meadows is still a pleasant country walk from the village.

Three modes of transport, *c.* 1926. While a lone walker uses the towing path, an Amblecote-bound tram emerges from woodland at The Hyde and a horse-drawn narrowboat, loaded with Black Country coal, heads towards Kidderminster and Stourport.

A variety of tramcars were used on the line. In the summer months, the quaintly named 'toast racks' – on account of their open sides – allowed passengers to breathe in the fresh air after leaving the Black Country.

When the line opened in 1901, the site of the former Hyde Iron Works was used as the railway's winter storage depot. A car is pictured about to leave The Hyde depot on a service run.

The Light Railway carried more than just passengers. This picture of the Kinver Terminus, c. 1908, shows milk churns about to be loaded into the car. To the left is the parcels and ticket office; by all accounts, an invaluable service for the quick and relatively cheap carriage of parcels and other small items was offered.

Tram Terminus, Kinver

Immediately the line opened, the village's fortunes changed for the better. With the collapse of the local iron industry, many families emigrated to the booming industry of the Black Country; some went even further – to the 'new worlds' of America, Canada, South Africa and Australia. For those remaining in Kinver, to work in Stourbridge or Amblecote meant walking or cycling at least 4 miles each way, there being no public transport. The line was an immediate success. Not only did it stem the tide of the population drifting away from the village but it brought many day trippers into Kinver – which the company's publicity literature described as 'the Switzerland of the Midlands'.

This picture was taken in about 1905, at the peak of the line's success in passenger numbers. On Whitsuntide Monday and Tuesday 1905, the line brought over 31,000 people into the village in a thirty-hour period. Contemporary reports tell of queues of homeward-bound day trippers stretching back into the High Street with trams travelling at seven-minute intervals. So popular had Kinver and 'The Edge' become that through services began running from places further afield such as Dudley and West Bromwich.

Thus Kinver took the first steps to becoming something of a 'dormitory' area for Black Country industry and commerce and a weekend-away-from-it-all resort. Indeed many industrialists built weekend cottages on the fringe of the village or bought existing houses there.

STAFFORDSHIRE &
WORCESTERSHIRE CANAL

The Staffordshire & Worcestershire Canal was part of James Brindley's 'Grand Cross' of canals linking the Severn, Trent, Mersey and Thames rivers together. It leaves the Trent & Mersey Canal at Great Haywood, near Stafford, and joins the River Severn at Stourport. Its opening in 1772 brought immediate economic benefits to Kinver in the form of cheaper bulk transport of raw materials such as coal, timber and other commodities.

With the opening of the Stourbridge Canal a few years later to Stourton Junction which, in turn, was connected to the Dudley Canal, the Staffordshire and Worcestershire Canal became one of the busiest and most prosperous waterways in the country as Black Country industry sent its goods to the Severn and on to Gloucester and Avonmouth Docks for export. Commercial carrying had all but ceased in 1950, but by 1960 privately owned and holiday hire-boats were making their appearance. By the 1990s the canal was once again one of the busiest on the waterway network and was carrying more pleasure craft than it did cargo boats 200 years before.

Hyde Lock and Cottage has always been one of the most popular subjects for artists and photographers and, apart from surrounding tree growth, has changed little over the last century. The house in the distance was once part of The Hyde Iron Works complex.

Equally timeless is Dunsley Dell, *c.* 1906, the bridle path from Dunsley to The Hyde, possibly an ancient pack-horse trail.

Kinver Lock, *c.* 1906. In front of the building on the right was a weighbridge whilst beyond that was the Lock Inn, believed to have been built shortly after the canal was opened in 1772, primarily as a boatman's pub. At the side of the later Vine Inn was an access road to a wharf operated by William Walker & Sons, which now forms part of the Vine Inn's beer garden. At a point behind the camera was a crane and wharf, while on the Dunsley side of the canal below the lock were another two wharves, reflecting the amount of waterborne trade from Kinver and district until around 1920 by which time road transport was becoming well established.

Shropshire Union Railway Boat *Wilden* pictured in about 1910 after having worked through Kinver Lock. The railway company concerned was the LNWR (later the LMS), which had taken control of the Shropshire Union Canal from Wolverhampton to Chester to give it a transport route through GWR territory.

A sign of the times, *c.* 1960. An unkempt Kinver Lock reflected the likelihood of the eventual closure of the canal by the British Transport Commission – a proposal which was rapidly withdrawn after a public outcry. Ironically, the boat pictured here was one of British Transport (Waterways) own holiday hire fleet.

This postcard view, *c.* 1930, of the canal from Kinver bridge shows in the foreground a 'day boat' owned by the Staffordshire, Worcestershire and Shropshire Electric Power Company (popularly known as the SWS), laden with coal and bound for the new power station at Stourport, opened in 1928. Because of their destination, all boats in this trade were known by boatmen as 'light boats' and were usually crewed by Black Countrymen who tied up at night either at Stourton or Kinver, went home by tram (and later, bus) returning early next morning to continue the journey, their horses usually being stabled locally. The coal came mainly from Ashwood Basin (now a boating marina) where the Earl of Dudley's private railway brought coal from his collieries to the canalside wharves. This traffic ceased almost overnight when, in 1948, following the nationalization of the railways and canals, all the coal traffic was switched to rail when British Railways opened a branch into the power station from the main line at Stourport.

How the area known as Gibraltar got its name is debatable. Possibly the outcrop of sandstone which became a cliff-face when the canal was cut had something to do with it, as the name was in existence in 1780. This scene of 1908 shows a number of houses perched on the hillside. According to a history of the local Methodist Church, the Wesleyans held services in a 'rock house' at Gibraltar in 1846, prior to which they had been holding meetings in the Lock Inn. By 1830 there were twelve rock houses, with seventeen being recorded in 1851. Many inhabitants were employed on the local canal wharves. Although the houses were deemed unhealthy in 1880, many continued to be used for a number of years by boatmen.

THE RIVER STOUR

Looking at the River Stour today, it is difficult, if not impossible, to imagine it as a navigable waterway. Yet in 1667 it was passable from Stourbridge to Kidderminster thanks to the efforts of Andrew Yarranton, and coal was carried from Stourbridge and Amblecote to Kidderminster.

Yarranton's plan was to make the river navigable to Lower Mitton in Stourport and he received Parliamentary approval for such a scheme in 1662. Finances ran out by the time he had reached Kidderminster and when, around 1670, a freak storm wrecked the navigation works, repairs were not undertaken and the navigation was abandoned.

For centuries the Stour's banks were home to many mills of various types and there were five in Kinver alone. Where weirs had been built to impound the water, the river was also used for pleasure boating. Eventually the weirs either collapsed or were removed and the river reverted to its natural state; years later extensive dredging saw spoil being piled against the banks making the river much narrower. At the same time industrial pollution from Black Country industries killed off all water life and the Stour had the dubious distinction of being one of the most polluted rivers in the country.

Today, however, thanks to anti-pollution measures, the river is slowly cleansing itself and several varieties of coarse fish have returned to its waters.

At the turn of the century Mr John Timmings operated a 'boating station' from the Mill Pool, Mill Lane. Unfortunately all boating activity ended when the mill weir deteriorated and the river level dropped. The site is now occupied by the Mill House sheltered accommodation for the elderly. The identities of the three men pictured are not known.

Mr Timmings's steam launch with passengers negotiating one of the many sharp bends in the river. Whilst a canopy can be seen protecting the helmsman and 'engineer' from the elements, the passengers did not seem to have such a luxury! Mr Timmings also ran a larger launch (below), which was capable of carrying up to twenty-five passengers.

A pleasant summer afternoon's boating and fishing on the Stour adjoining the village. A far cry from today's narrow river channel and high banks.

The river level at Kinver can rise rapidly at times of heavy rainfall in the Stour Valley and, as this photograph taken from near the Lock Inn around 1920 shows, flood water closed Mill Lane to all except horsedrawn traffic.

The old river bridge with the Stag Inn in the background, *c.* 1910.

With the increasing number and size of vehicles travelling in and out of Kinver, it became evident that a wider and stronger bridge was needed. This work was carried out in 1921.

The new bridge ready for the onslaught of the motor car. . . .

HIGH STREET

K inver village was described by Stebbing Shaw in 'History and Antiquities of Staffordshire', in 1798 as 'one long spacious street well paved with pebbles'. Over 500 years earlier Kinver had been given a formal Borough Charter, and as there are no records of that title ever having been removed, Kinver could still feasibly refer to itself as a Borough.

That 'one long spacious street' also encompassed the Borough and eventually became known as High Street; today its architecture spans some 500 years and not even the continual presence of road traffic can completely overcome that sense of history.

As will be revealed in the following pages, many of the properties have their own stories to tell. Collectively these stories are the history of a village.

By the time this postcard appeared in 1923, Kinver was a well-established tourist venue. This view of High Street, taken from the junction of Church Hill and Mill Lane, shows 'E. Guttery' offering teas and 'apartments' — obviously in competition with the Temperance Hotel next door. These two properties were demolished around 1946.

Further evidence of enterprising Kinver residents cashing in on the early 20th-century tourist boom. On the right is Kemp's Refreshment and Tea Rooms, roughly on the site of today's Spar Supermarket. On the left, three of the four villas (which still exist) were offering tourist facilities including accommodation.

The name 'Burgesses', by which this house was known, dates back several hundred years to the time when the Lord of the Manor issued a 'Charter of Liberties for his Burgesses', and at the same time created the Borough of Kinver. The Borough was an area of land encompassing what is now both sides of the High Street. The house was demolished in the early 1960s but its name was retained for the area now occupied by sheltered accommodation for the elderly.

Apart from the disappearance of the Temperance Hotel on the right and the cottages on the left, the remainder of the High Street has changed little since this photograph from the mid-1930s.

High Street viewed from outside the Constitutional Club, *c.* 1960. Absent from today's street scene is the Co-operative Society Store on the right.

High Street in 1909, and the only vehicles in sight are a horsedrawn cart and, on the right-hand pavement a pedal cycle. The building in the centre background was built in 1851 as a National School for Boys and Girls. A separate school for girls was built in 1873; the building is now the library. A boys' school was built in Castle Street and the older building then used as an infants' school.

One of the most distinctive façades of any property in High Street is The Pharmacy. For 140 years it has been the village's pharmacy, while for over fifty years the other section of the building (right) was the village post office – as seen in this picture, *c.* 1910. Previously the post office had been at 33 High Street, moving to the Pharmacy building in around 1908.

A photograph (above) taken some fifty years later shows little change apart from a weighing machine outside Mr Bills's Pharmacy and a post office sign. With the growth in demand for telephones in Kinver in the 1950s, the telephone exchange became overloaded and a new fully automatic exchange was built at Dunsley. A mobile crane was then used to remove the old exchange equipment (below) via a first floor window.

Possibly a Saturday afternoon in 1911, with people enjoying a stroll down an almost traffic-free High Street. Many would have been day-trippers who had come to Kinver on the Light Railway from the Black Country. This postcard could have been a publicity photograph for the newsagent, Mr Jennings, whose name on the shop blind seems to have been enhanced for the benefit of clarity. Although this card was published in about 1920, it is a reprint of a 1911 postcard when the newsagent's shop blind carried the name 'Morgan'. To the right of centre foreground can be seen a uniformed man, possibly the village police constable. The very wide road and pavements at this point, the junction of High Street and Vicarage Drive, mark the area in which the village Bull Ring was situated and also the site of the 17th-century Market House, which, by all accounts, was short-lived.

An almost deserted High Street in 1906 gives a clear view of the ancient frontage of the White Harte Hotel which, as licensed premises, has existed since 1605. High Street once carried the main Bristol–Chester road and the White Harte was a well-patronized hostelry. Evidence of Civil War activity around Kinver is well documented and, during restoration work at the hotel, a Cromwellian helmet was discovered. In the early 19th century the hotel was the venue for the 'Borough Meeting' and in 1830 there are records of a 'White Harte Club', which may have been an early version of a Friendly Society.

Despite substantial local opposition, the Alms Houses in High Street were demolished in the 1960s and replaced with a modern shop development. Ten years later such demolition would have been unlikely as the centre of the village had been designated a conservation area.

The date of this picture is unknown but it could be of a parade marking the end of the Second World War. To the right, the group of marching men may have been either Auxiliary Police ('Specials'), Auxiliary Fire Service or Air Raid Wardens. Behind them are drummers wearing what appears to have been army uniforms – could they be the Home Guard? Kinver Historical Society would be grateful if anyone could identify the occasion.

For years Mr Archie Taylor was the village's hairdresser; he was also the founder of the Village Band. Stories are told of customers being attended to while band practice proceeded in a back room and then having to wait while Mr Taylor rushed into the practice room to berate some hapless bandsman for blowing a wrong note!

Kinver Tea Stores receiving a delivery of provisions, *c.* 1905. The wagon was owned by a Joseph Norton of Wolverhampton. (Facing page, top) The Tea Stores had been taken over by Mr Sid Phillips, pictured here in 1958 demonstrating the ultimate in customer service by giving Pauline Beebee a 'piggy-back' across the flooded High Street. Mrs Phillips is seen in the side entry door. (Below) An internal view of the shop, with Mrs Dorothy Day serving Mrs I. Williams, *c.* 1960.

A view of High Street looking towards Church Hill, *c.* 1910.

The first of many newsagents (Morgan, Jennings and now Stars News Shops) was Miss Dorothy Ellen Lizzie Taylor. This photograph of about 1914 shows the newspaper billboard announcing the size of the German army and the declaration of war.

High Street, 1964 (above). The building on the extreme right was formerly the Red Lion pub, later changing to an English and now a Chinese restaurant.

The cottages and shops on the left were demolished and the land used for a car-park. In 1992 and in the teeth of some local opposition, the Normid Housing Association built a block of apartments here, which won an architecture and design award as well as an award from the Kinver Civic Society.

Although not in the High Street, Harris's Garage of Stone Lane was strategically placed on the main route used by motorists and cyclists heading towards Kinver Edge from High Street. Mr Harris lost no time in offering parking for cars and motorcycle combinations for 6*d*, motor cycles 4*d* and cycles 2*d*. He also served refreshments. His petrol was delivered by hand operated pumps. Note the sign 'battery charging station' – the days when, before everyone had electricity, people with wireless sets powered them by accumulators which were charged from the mains supply.

LICENSED PREMISES

Although being classed as a large village with a population of around 8,000, the original village's central area has retained much of its character by reason of the river and a backdrop of hills.

As a result – and because of the influx of visitors which is now experienced throughout the year rather than in just the summer months – comparatively few pubs have closed down.

In recent years Kinver gained national fame when it was listed by CAMRA Real Ale Guide as well worth a visit for good quality and value. Most of the pubs now provide meals and, as the village's tourist trade has increased, a number of licensed restaurants have become established, two of which began life as pubs.

Arguably the best-known hostelry from a historical point of view within Kinver parish is the Whittington Inn standing on the A449 Kidderminster–Wolverhampton road. But it was not until the 18th century that it became licensed property; before that it was the manor house of the De Whittingtons, having been built in about 1310. Richard, a grandson of the first owner, eventually became Lord Mayor of London on four occasions. His background of some aristocracy destroys the story of him arriving in London, poor and penniless, with his cat and then making his fortune.

The Inn has several links with royalty: Lady Jane Grey spent some of her childhood there; King Charles II is reputed to have stayed there during his flight from Worcester (Kinver is one place where he didn't climb a tree!); and in 1711 Queen Anne called and, as was her custom when staying overnight, left her iron seal (since stolen) on the door.

The interior of the Whittington Inn is what today's traveller would expect from a building of such antiquity. Above is the heavily timbered lounge hall whilst below is the bedroom used by Lady Jane Grey when she lived there as a child. Her ghost is said to still roam the corridors. . . .

The Stag Inn, Mill Lane when a Mr J. Blakeway, Home Brewer, was the licensee, *c.* 1904. It has long since been demolished. The inn was conveniently situated almost opposite the Kinver Light Railway terminus. Beyond the Stag is a row of cottages standing against the sandstone cliff adjoining The Holloway. The occupants carved caves out of the sandstone and used them as outhouses and storerooms. With the cottages long gone, the caves can now be seen in their entirety.

White Hill in 1917 was a scene of almost open countryside. The building to the right was formerly The Spring Gardens, rebuilt as pictured as The Spring. In about 1938 it was demolished and replaced by The New Rose & Crown to serve the growing residential development of Kinver. The land in the immediate foreground and almost up to the skyline was completely built over by the 1970s.

Formerly the Car & Horses, this building predated the arrival of the motor car by many years despite its name, the only explanation being that the word car was merely short for 'carriage'. It was completely refurbished as a house which became known as The Armoury, on the grounds that it had some connection with the Civil War – a claim that has never been substantiated either by artefacts or documentary evidence. This photograph is dated from around 1895.

The Green Dragon in High Street, seen above in about 1898, was first licensed in 1718. In about 1902 it was rebuilt as an upmarket hotel in anticipation of an influx of residential bookings which never materialized. In 1936 it became the Constitutional Club, its exterior virtually the same today – as depicted in the 1905 postcard below.

The Red Lion, today a Chinese restaurant, stood on the corner of what is now the access road to the public car-park known locally as The Acre. The photograph was taken pre-1900, for in 1896 Kelly's Directory named George Boswell as the licensee. With the Union Flag (Union Jack) flying, this photograph could have been taken at the time of Queen Victoria's Golden Jubilee of 1897. In 1900, Kelly's Directory named Giblum Grimshaw as licensee. At the rear of the Red Lion a Mr Underwood offered 'good stabling'. From the car-park a footpath leads up to the parish church.

High Street from near the Vine Café, *c.* 1895.

This 1912 postcard view of a near deserted High Street also heralded the arrival of road transport as a delivery van trundles past the Crown Inn on the left; this is now the Kinfayre Restaurant.

Known locally as 'The Steps' was the Mitchells and Butlers Pub, the Plough & Harrow, High Street as seen, *c.* 1950. It is now a Batham's House, well known for its real ale, Bathams being one of the few surviving true Black Country breweries. Next door (extreme right) can be seen the bricked-up window arch of the former Baptist chapel built in 1814. The chapel became an Anglican Sunday School in 1827, was returned to the Baptists in 1834 and was later let to the Primitive Methodists who remained there until 1839. Eventually it was converted into retail premises.

The Royal Exchange, Enville Road, *c.* 1912, was the setting for the group photograph above; whether it was a special event or merely a gathering of the 'regulars' is not recorded. The Royal Exchange was also known locally as 'The Cherry Tree' as can be seen from the photograph below, *c.* 1918, when Kinver was beginning to receive visits from motorists.

CHURCHES

From its hilltop position, the parish church dominates the village. It is possible that the area could have been a place of pagan worship before the arrival of Christianity. It is known that there was a priest in Kinver in 1086, although it was not until the 12th century that there was any record of a church building. Some of the present church's original Norman stonework still exists.

The hilltop position of the parish church can be seen perfectly in this 1930s postcard.

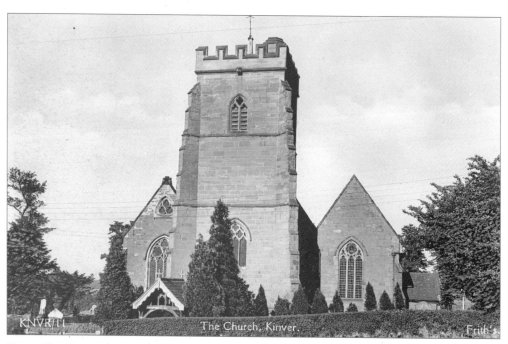

Kinver Church, seen here in about 1938, appears to have been rebuilt in the early 14th century and only fragments of stone survive from an earlier Norman construction. Over the past 600 years many alterations have been carried out on the building, a major external job being the demolition of the north aisle (left) in 1976, which had become structurally unsafe. It was replaced to a design by Mr J.G. Smith of Kinver.

In 1878 a restoration scheme was undertaken and spread over a number of years, the work finally being completed for Queen Victoria's Golden Jubilee celebrations in 1887. At the same time as the north aisle was being rebuilt in 1976, the wooden ceiling of the nave was removed to uncover the medieval roof.

Trinity Church (Wesleyan Methodist) was built in High Street in 1887 to a design by Isaac Meacham of Cradley Heath, who also designed the Sunday School Hall which was opened in 1889. The church closed in the early 1960s with the congregation joining the Methodists of Potter's Cross, Kinver. The buildings were then occupied for a time by youth organizations, but the cost of maintenance and the unwelcome attentions of local vandals led to demolition in 1995. The site was redeveloped as retirement homes.

At the turn of the century, the Primitive Methodists obtained land at the junction of Meddins Lane and Enville Road, Potter's Cross, and built a chapel measuring 30 ft by 18 ft and made of corrugated metal sheeting. In this postcard view of Potter's Cross, *c.* 1920, the tiny chapel can be seen above the hedgerow. In 1924 the congregation built Christ Church on adjoining land in 1924, with the chapel then becoming a Sunday School.

KNVR.118.   NEW METHODIST CHAPEL. KINVER.

The then modern style of church architecture can be seen in the Methodist Church, Potter's Cross, which was opened in 1961. With the closure of the Wesleyan Methodist Church, it became known as Kinver Methodist Church. Much of the cost of the new building came from a bequest made by Mr F. Payne of Norton, Stourbridge.

PRINCIPAL HOUSES

As becomes a long-established community set within particularly attractive rural surroundings, Kinver had several large and prestigious houses, many dating back several centuries and almost all of which remain in existence. Owners over the last 200 years reflect the popularity of Kinver amongst the successful industrialists, first those of the local ironworking industry and later, as transport links improved, of the Black Country. Several smaller houses were built by Black Country businessmen as weekend and holiday homes.

The origins of Prestwood House, situated off the A449 Wolverhampton–Kidderminster road, have been traced back to the reign of Richard III when it was occupied by John De Somery. It is said that even before this period the area was associated with members of a monastic order attached to the monastery at Wolverhampton. Over the centuries, many famous local families occupied and added to the house, among them being the Dudleys, Lytteltons, Sebrights, Hodgsons and Foleys. At the end of its life as a grand residence it became a sanatorium for victims of tuberculosis. It is now a private nursing home.

Prestwood House was, naturally, the venue for many social events such as the Hunt Meet (above) and a Rook Shoot (below), where a house party pose complete with their 'bag', *c.* 1907. The occupant of the house at that time was Mr George Salter, who can be seen at the centre of the front row.

Prestwood Estate covered a substantial area, and in this picture Miss Salter (left) is pictured with Miss Savery and a companion in a donkey cart before a morning ride, *c.* 1908.

The impressive Victorian and Edwardian furnishings of Mrs Salter's drawing room at Prestwood House, *c.* 1910.

In 1316, Dunsley Hall, situated on a rocky outcrop overlooking the Stour Valley was the manor house of Gilbert le Dunsley. The present building, pictured in 1918, still contains some of the original building's timbers. In 1812, its then owner, Benjamin Robins, was murdered by a travelling carpenter who was subsequently traced, arrested, tried and executed at Stafford. His body was brought back to the scene of the crime, a local wood, and 'gibbeted' – placed in an iron cage – and hung from a tree for twelve months. Not surprisingly the area became known as Gibbet Wood, and the track to Stourbridge Gibbet Lane.

STOURTON CASTLE. FRONT ENTRANCE DRIVE.

(Opposite) Stourton Castle began life as a Royal Hunting Lodge probably in the 11th century when it is reputed that King William II was in Kinver. Since then it has had links with a number of kings and their courts, namely Henry II, John, Edward IV, Henry VII and Henry VIII. Cardinal Pole was born at the castle in 1500, but after falling out of favour with Henry VIII spent some time abroad. On one occasion it was reported that he declined the election as Pope. As Archbishop of Canterbury, says Arthur Mee (*The King's England – Staffordshire*), Pole was implicated in 'religious persecutions of violence and horror' during Queen Mary's reign.

During the Civil War Stourton appeared to adopt a neutral role, but after the Cromwellians took it over Royalist forces from Worcester routed the Cromwellians at Stourbridge Heath and claimed the castle for the King. After a chequered career in turbulent times, the castle was then occupied by tenants and owners who were all either pioneers in the iron-working industry which sprang up in the Stour Valley or, in later years, were leaders in the industrial and commercial life of the Black Country. Today the castle remains in private hands. The best view of the castle and its gardens is from the towpath of the Staffordshire & Worcestershire Canal.

Dunsley House was built in the early 1800s and, as 'Dunsley Villa', was occupied by the Hancox family until the mid-1860s. It was used as a rest home by the Girls' Friendly Society from 1912 until the 1930s.

Rockmount, Dark Lane, was the birthplace of Kinver's most famous daughter, actress and author Nancy Price. It was built in or before 1624; in 1672 it became known as The Stone House and, in the 1860s, Rockmount. In her autobiography *Into an Hour Glass,* Nancy tells of the ghost of a former vicar of Kinver the Revd John Newley, that haunted the house. What the vicar's connections were with the house have never been recorded.

Nancy Price was born in Kinver in 1880. Her father, William Henry Price and her grandfather ran a prosperous canal haulage company in Brierley Hill and played a major part in forming what was to become one of the largest canal carrying fleets in England – Fellows, Morton & Clayton Ltd. From an early age she was destined for an illustrious stage career and became widely regarded as one of England's finest character actresses. Despite her success on the London stage, she never lost her affection for Kinver. In addition to her stage career as an actress and eventually a producer, she wrote several books and in one she wrote: 'Almost every sixth dream is about Kinver, my old home and the Church there.' In 1950 she was awarded the CBE for her services to the theatre. She died in 1970, aged ninety.

Nancy Price's wedding in 1907 was probably the social event of the year for Kinver with the reception being held literally on two levels in the magnificent gardens of the family home. In the upper garden, family and personal friends were seated at individual tables and in this picture several have been identified. The bride and bridegroom, Mr Charles Maude, are pictured on the right. Seated (second left) is Mr Cole, the Grammar School headmaster and behind him is Mr Raglan Neale, the proprietor of the White Harte Hotel. To Mr Cole's immediate left is Mrs Alice Bills and Mr Albert James Bills, village chemist, and seated (extreme right) is Miss Dorothy Bills.

In the lower garden and seated at a long table were Mr Price's employees and their partners who had presumably made the journey to Kinver on the Light Railway. The uniformed bandsmen are thought to have come from Stourbridge.

Old Grammar School House was the village's grammar school from the late 1550s until it closed down through lack of money and pupils in around 1913. The school's origins can be traced back to 1511 when the local priest was instructed to 'teach Grammar to Kinver children'. Whilst the date of founding is unknown, it was one of many Chantry schools closed down by Edward VI. When the King later granted a number of charters for grammar schools, Kinver was not included; the nearest was King Edward VI School, Stourbridge. Local people then raised sufficient money to found the village's own grammar school and it continued successfully for around 350 years.

Formerly Hyde House, this 17th-century building was first owned by the Foley family of Hyde Iron Works and retained connections with the local iron industry until 1880. In 1906 the Revd E.G. Hexall, supported by voluntary contributions, renamed the house 'Bethany' and used it as a home where crippled children, some abandoned as babies by their parents, were educated and taught a trade within their physical capabilities. In seven years the home was caring for and training forty physically handicapped boys. It closed in about 1918 and a few years later the building was demolished. No trace of it remains.

THE VILLAGE FRINGE

Although the High Street was, and still is, at the heart of the village, on its outskirts are many features which, individually and collectively, have given Kinver its unique character.

As will be seen in the following pictures, open farmland that once stretched up to Kinver Edge has been built over, most of the development having taken place after 1950. This development was in response to the number of people wishing to move out of the West Midlands conurbation and live in a country area yet remain within easy reach of employment.

Periodically, developers attempt to spread outwards but the designated green belt surrounding the village, if retained, will ensure that Kinver remains at about its present size and will not suffer the fate of so many other Midland villages, which have become dormitory areas for the larger towns.

Now a private residence called Clifford Cottage, the workhouse on Church Hill was the second such establishment in Kinver. The first one was recorded in 1739 when three cottages in Swan Lane, later Vicarage Drive, were leased to the parish for twenty-one years and converted into a workhouse. By 1830 the workhouse had moved to Church Hill.

At the rear and to the side of Clifford Cottage was the old prison, the bulk of which had been excavated from the sandstone cliff and faced with brick as shown in this 1905 view.

Approaching the village down Dunsley Road was to travel down a country lane through open countryside. At the bottom of the hill can be seen the Vine Inn with Church Hill in the background. This photograph dates from about 1930.

Looking down The Holloway, a narrow track hewn out of sandstone between Church Hill and Mill Lane, c. 1920. At the top of The Holloway was the Catholic church, once a former school. The church closed in the 1980s.

Church Hill at its junction with Cookley Lane, *c.* 1915.

The same junction, this time looking towards Cookley, with a motorcycle combination heralding the forthcoming invasion of motor transport, *c.* 1920.

Foster Street (named after James Foster, a Stourbridge iron master and tenant of Stourton Castle) as seen in about 1926 from the playground of the former junior school in Enville Road, with Kinver Edge dominating the skyline. The houses were built and funded by an earlier Friendly Society in about 1850.

Potter's Cross and the 'Doll's Houses', so named because of their external appearance, in 1918. The fields to the right are now occupied by a number of shops, as seen below in 1950. The open fields in the background (right) are colonized by a large housing development built in the 1960s.

Meddins Lane and Kinver Edge.

Viewed from Potter's Cross today, all the farmland seen bordering Meddins Lane in this 1916 postcard view has been covered with housing. Kinver Edge, mainly because it was used for grazing, carried very few trees. The four villas, including the shop, are still in existence as is the building (right background) which, for many years, was a small general store known as 'Ison's; much of its custom, including afternoon teas, came from day trippers.

Meddins Lane, Kinver.

The building of Council houses in 1930 marked the beginning of widespread housing development in the Potter's Cross, Meddins Lane and White Hill areas.

Enville Road from Potter's Cross, *c.* 1950, is not vastly different from today's street scene.

Hyde Lane looking towards Enville Road, *c.* 1950. The Edge in the background shows an increase in tree cover from that seen in earlier photographs.

Heathlands (Enville Road) looking towards Enville in 1917 – a scene that has changed little in 100 years.

This is another picture on which the Historical Society would like more information. Before the war, fairs regularly visited Kinver and one site was in what is now Fairfield Drive. The location of this one is not known.

Since the early part of this century Kinver has been a popular area for Scout and Guide activities. The pine woods which surround the Compa campsite are an ideal woodcraft training area, as seen in this 1913 photograph of a Scoutmaster and his young charges.

The Log Cabin was built in 1933 and opened on 3 June of that year by Lady Baden Powell. The entrance to the campsite was 'guarded' by the two totem poles shown below. Those pictured have been replaced. The site was provided by the Webb family for use by the Worcestershire Scout Association at a peppercorn rent and was sold to the Association in 1994.

TOTEM POLES, KINVER SCOUT CAMP   M 5988

Kinver was also a popular camping area for the Boys' Brigade, seen here on parade passing the Elizabethan House in High Street. The date of this event is unknown. The house has been undergoing restoration by the West Midlands Historic Buildings Trust and in 1996 received financial assistance from the National Lottery.

Kinver has always been a lively community ready to celebrate any event of national or local importance; one such enthusiastic organization was the 'Kinver Jubilee Jazzers'. This picture could have been for the 1935 Jubilee but any information would be welcomed by Kinver Historical Society.

TOURISM

The unspoilt countryside, woodland and the open heathland of Kinver Edge has been a magnet for visitors from the Black Country for over a century. In the earliest days of Kinver as a tourism attraction, visitors were usually those fortunate enough to have their own horse and carriage or able to afford the relatively high cost of hiring a horse 'brake'.

When the Light Railway opened, Kinver experienced instant success as a day or half-day destination. By the time the railway closed in 1930, Kinver had a regular bus service to Stourbridge and coach operators had found Kinver a popular venue.

Today Kinver remains a favourite place among West Midlanders even though the motor car and motorways enable families to travel further afield for a day out. Happily Kinver has escaped much of the brash and intrusive commercialization that has ruined many other rural destinations.

Winding up from the village towards Kinver Edge, the tourism 'trail' was well established by 1910. This postcard scene is of Museum Cottages in The Compa and their tea garden and shelter, *c.* 1920.

ROCK HOUSE MUSEUM, KINVER.

Adjoining the cottage and tea garden was the Rock House Museum. This former sandstone dwelling was run by the owner, Mr Fairbridge (pictured with his cat), for some twenty years complete with a selection of the forerunners of today's one-armed bandits.

Nearby was another tourism enterprise, Martindale's Tea Rooms and Gardens. On the extreme right can be seen a large tea room sign which also advertised overnight accommodation for members of the Cyclists Touring Club.

The Compa and road junction looking from Church Hill, *c*. 1910. To the left is the road leading up to Edge View Hotel, Tea Rooms and Kinver Edge. To the right, a public footpath still leads to what is now Fairfield Drive. It was a well-trodden route used by the multitude of visitors going to and from the village centre and the Light Railway terminus. In the foreground is one of several groups of gaming machines so popular in cafés at that time.

Without doubt the largest single commercial enterprise in the village in the early part of the century was the Edge View Hotel in the Compa. In this scene, *c.* 1906, it was well patronized by day-trippers as well as residents. To the right can be seen the hotel's Café Royale tea room with seating for over 300 people. The enterprise eventually went bankrupt, its failure being blamed on the refusal of the local Licensing Justices to allow it to sell alcohol! It then became a sanatorium (linked to Prestwood Sanitorium) for the treatment of tuberculosis; it was said that the air around the surrounding pine woods contained healing properties for chest complaints. After several years and the virtual eradication of tuberculosis, it was used as a recovery and convalescence home. Another change of use saw it converted into a home for mentally handicapped people. In the 1970s, it was closed down and at the date of this publication a proposal had been made to convert it into a private nursing home.

The former Edge View Hotel as a tuberculosis hospital in 1920.

After the failure of the Edge View Hotel, the Wells family opened tea rooms on what is now Fairfield Drive, off Stone Lane. Adjoining ground, now occupied by Foley Infants' School, soon became a well-used coach park as can be seen from this picture of people making their way back to the tea rooms and coaches, *c.* 1930. Several of the coaches pictured are believed to have been operated by Samuel Johnson 'Supreme' of Stourbridge, with others, including the one in the centre with a white roof, operated by Midland Red probably from the company's Foster Street garage in Stourbridge.

KINVER EDGE.

As Kinver grew in popularity among day-trippers, there were also many who bought small plots of land nearer Kinver Edge and the woodland and built small chalets or cottages as holiday homes. This photograph, *c.* 1918, shows a number of such chalets and cottages in the area now occupied by Church View Gardens, Compton Gardens and Compton Road. Needless to say, such development was before Town and Country Planning legislation had been enacted.

Sandy Lane, leading from the top of Kinver Edge and the National Trust Warden's cottage to Blakeshall, is now a heavily-used road particularly on summer weekends and is a far cry from this early 1920s scene, when it was what its name suggested.

The wide open space of Kinver Edge and the 'Eleven Apostles' – a clump of trees – as seen in about 1920. The 'Roman Encampment' referred to on the postcard is, in fact, the earthwork ramparts of an Iron Age Fort which in recent years have been cleared of scrub to reveal the extent of the fortification ditches.

ROCK HOUSES

A major attraction to Kinver for generations has been its cluster of Rock Houses. The earliest record of habitation was in 1814 when the burial was recorded of a woman, aged seventy-four, who had lived there. In 1914 there were about fourteen families living in the Rock Houses but by the 1950s all the families had been rehoused, although one house continued to be used as a café until 1967.

The frequently held view that the Rock Houses had been developed from prehistoric caves has never been proven. Certainly the dwellings nearest the village were on the site of an old sandstone quarry, which fell into disuse when it was found the sandstone was too soft to be of use in construction work. However, it was easy to fashion into living rooms which were warm in winter and cool in summer.

While many of the remains of the Rock Houses in the Kinver area now lie on private land, a group of them are now in National Trust ownership. The Trust has restored one group as an exact copy of the original houses; local Trust volunteers cleared a substantial area of scrubland and returned it to the type of cultivation which existed at the turn of the century.

This postcard view, *c.* 1908, shows Mrs Charlotte Shaw in the garden of one of the 'top level' rock houses, with the stone and tile extensions hiding other rooms carved out of the sandstone.

A view of the Holy Austin rock houses and gardens as seen from Compton Road, *c.* 1903.

On the 'bottom level', c. 1910. This house was lived in by Mr and Mrs Fletcher in 1900, and they are featured in a painting by Alfred Rushton which now hangs in the Constitutional Club, Kinver.

Another resident of one of the 'bottom level' rock houses, c. 1915. The only major change from the picture above is the renewed wooden frame at the well-head.

Also on the bottom level and facing Stone Lane and Compton Road, this rock house, *c.* 1910, had the unusual feature of the living-room chimney brickwork following the contour of the cliff face. This house was the setting of the 1919 film 'Bladys of the Stewponey', which was financed by a Kinver man and Black Country industrialist, Benjamin Priest.

Mrs Martindale making lace at her rock house home, *c.* 1910.

Nanny's Rock, *c.* 1928. There is no evidence that this was ever used as a dwelling in the accepted sense of the word, for in its five chambers there is no sign of door or window frames having been installed. However, one of the caves was known as 'Mag-o'-Fox' hole, *c.* 1680, a name which may have been derived from the name of a woman 'Margaret of the Fox Earth' who was said to have lived there and whose death was recorded in 1617. When this photograph was taken, generations of sightseers had carved their initials in the sandstone.

A general view of Nanny's Rock, *c.* 1914. How the outcrop gained this name has never been satisfactorily explained, unless one of the caves may have been used centuries ago by a hermit. This suggestion, like many others, may be based purely on supposition or just pure romanticism. . . .

HERE & THERE: A MISCELLANY OF THE VILLAGE COMMUNITY

U nlike many communities, Kinver has managed to retain its own identity and in many ways has developed a highly distinctive and independent image. It can be argued that it has more social, occupational and sporting activities than many other communities of similar or even larger size.

Although retaining its basically rural character, the community has successfully kept pace with developments in the modern lifestyle, without becoming a commuter overspill satellite of the West Midlands conurbation.

The village has a tradition of good educational facilities which date back to over 400 years ago, when the inhabitants financed their own grammar school. Although that school has now closed, others have continued to flourish.

Today, there are at least seventy individual organizations in the village including activities as varied as drama, local history studies, horticulture, music, wine-making, the Arts Festival, cricket, football and model engineering. Examples in the following pages of this collective and individual energy going back nearly a century are, in themselves, proof of a successful self-contained rural community, which few want to leave and many want to join.

This picture of Kingsford Lane, *c.* 1908, is reminiscent of a Constable painting and is a far cry from today's Kingsford Lane. Although the area is heavily wooded there are now numerous car-parks and picnic areas forming part of the Kingsford Country Park.

On the other side of Kinver Edge from Kingsford Lane is Blakeshall Lane, pictured here in 1910. One family enjoys the 'freedom' of the motor car.

Management, staff and VIPs line up for the photographer in 1908 at the opening of the Mill Lane
Waterworks, from an original photograph in the Kinver Historical Society archives. The site is now
occupied by Mill House.

Pipe laying in The Holloway, *c.* 1910.

Sewerage pipes being laid at The Compa in the 1920s, reflecting the expansion of development away from the village centre. The Martindale and other tea rooms can be seen in the background.

A traction engine hauling timber in Kinver early this century (date unknown). The engine, according to a sign on its boiler, belonged to an Amblecote haulage contractor.

Steam power on the farm. A stationary steam engine at work driving a threshing machine during harvest time on a Kinver farm. Although no date is known, it could have been in the 1890s as the engine itself was horse drawn.

A local farmer, Mr S. Piper, proudly displays his prize certificate awarded for his cow, c. 1911.

The largest fox ever killed in Britain and recorded in the *Guinness Book of Records* was this one shot at Lydiatts Coppice, Greyfields Estate, on 11 March 1956. It weighed 28 lbs 2 oz, was 54 inches long from nose to tail and stood 21 inches high at the shoulder.

Kinver fire engine outside the George and Dragon, High Street whilst taking part in the 1936 Silver Jubilee celebration parade. At one time the village's chemist, Mr Frank Bills, was the local brigade's chief officer.

With the outbreak of the Second World War this Lanchester saloon car was converted into a fire tender. The rear panels were cut away and seating installed for the crew. It pulled a trailer on which was loaded a high capacity water pump. Although also used to fight local fires, it was, happily, never called on to fight the effects of enemy action in the village. The cost of conversion was met by money left over from the village's 1937 Coronation Fund.

Kinver Boys' Council School sports prizewinners, *c.* 1910, and (below) another group of sports winners from the same school in 1912.

A group of pupils from Kinver Boys' Council School with their Headmaster Mr A.L. Shepherd, *c.* 1912.

Group 2 from Kinver Infants' School with their teacher, Miss Angel, *c.* 1910.

The whole of the Boys' Council School assembled for this picture in 1913.

Kinver Football Club with an unidentified trophy in the 1948–9 season. A number of the team have been identified. Back row, left to right: Bill Taylor, George Hadley, Jack Lane, -?-, ? Timmins, Bob Glover, Tony Jordan. Front row: ? Saunders, -?-, -?-. M. Fitton -?-, and ? Saunders.

The day the FA Cup came to Kinver in 1954. Through the good offices of former West Bromich Albion star Arthur Fitton, who later became Kinver's National Trust warden, the village had a sight of that famous trophy. It was won by 'The Baggies' with a 3–2 victory over Preston North End on May 1 of that year.

A dinner of the Royal Antedeluvian Order of Buffaloes at the Green Dragon (later the Constitutional Club), *c.* 1917. What the event was is not recorded.

A children's 'street party' at the rear of the Old Plough celebrates the 1953 Coronation.

The Kinver tourist trade of the early 20th century made maximum use of the seaside-style of comic postcards for visitors to send to relatives and friends. Some were of the typical 'wish-you-were-here' style while others were, for those days, somewhat 'saucy'. Here are two examples of the more 'respectable' ones.

'Business as usual' (facing page, above and overleaf). In the darkest days of the Second World War, September 1941, Kinver village businesses did their best to appear as if nothing had changed, as can be seen from these advertisements which appeared in the Parish Church magazine.

ENVILLE

E nville village is one of the few villages remaining close to the West Midlands conurbation that has escaped the spread of suburbia. This is due, no doubt, to the surrounding green belt. Much of the area is within the Enville Hall estate and the village lies within a conservation area.

The village has remained a closely knit community over the centuries. The parish as a whole comprises a number of isolated farmhouses and cottages which reflect their origins within the Kinver Forest.

Totally rural, Enville parish once comprised three manors – the Anglo-Saxon settlements of Enville and Morfe – with Lutley being first mentioned in the 12th century.

Straddling the Stourbridge–Bridgnorth road, the village centre lies at the foot of a ridge on the summit of which stands the parish church.

Adjoining the village is Enville Hall which has remained in the same family for over 400 years. In the Hall grounds is the cricket field; laid in 1821 it was regarded at the time as superior to Lord's. The first match was played in 1821 and has been played there ever since.

Enville parish church as seen today is the result of a substantial restoration by Sir Gilbert Scott between 1872 and 1874, when substantial internal and external work was carried out including the reconstruction of the tower. Standing on a ridge alongside the Bridgnorth Road, the church occupies a dominant position above the village and although there is no record of when the first church was built, architectural evidence indicates the existence of a church on this site by the 12th century. The Church of St Mary was an invocation in use by the 18th century although in the 16th century the name St Laurence was in use. Earlier, in the Middle Ages, there was an altar dedicated to St Nicholas. Nonconformity flourished for only a short time in the village. In 1855 a house in the village was opened for use by the Wesleyan Methodists, but about two years later the meetings were abandoned because of opposition by the Rector, Cornelius Jesson.

Interior of Enville Church.

A view of Enville village from the parish church, looking towards Kinver.

The picturesque approach to Enville along the Stourbridge road as seen here, about seventy years ago, has hardly changed today apart from a wider carriageway.

Stamford House was built in 1857 as the Stamford Arms Hotel to cater for visitors to the Hall gardens and cricket festivals. It closed in 1892 when the gardens were no longer open to the public and it became a private residence. It was demolished in 1950.

The village war memorial was erected on a triangular piece of land (see previous picture) adjoining the road to the Hall. This photograph may have been taken at the memorial's dedication, date unknown.

Enville Village with Blundies Lane to the left, *c.* 1905. Beyond the buildings (which included a shop) stood the village school, which was opposite the Cat Inn.

Looking towards Bridgnorth, the parish church tower can be seen on the ridge overlooking the village.

The Cat Inn, *c.* 1903. First mentioned in 1777, this was one of two inns in that period, the other being the Swan Inn. Another inn, The Crown, was known to exist in 1642 but there is a suggestion that it may have existed as early as 1582. Still a popular hostelry, The Cat Inn is unusual in that it only retains a six day licence. It never opens on a Sunday.

Avenue, Enville Hall   Valentines Series

Enville Hall is the predominant feature of the village, the economic welfare of which was almost totally dependent on the Hall and its vast estate. Before the conquest, the manor was held by Alric, a King's thegn. The manor passed through several hands until, in 1528, Lord Dudley sold it to Sir Edward Grey of Whittington, Kinver, whose descendants still own it. No trace of the original manor house remains. It was replaced in around 1548 by a new house built by Grey. Over the ensuing 400 years, the Hall has had many additions and its gardens, of some 60 acres, were described in the 1880s as some of the finest in the country. The Hall eventually became the home of the Earl of Stamford and Warrington. The title became extinct in 1883 with the death of the seventh Earl and ownership was passed down through the female line. Pictured below is the tree-lined drive to the Hall from the Kinver Road, the main entrance being from the village centre.

Enville Hall, North Front.

The north front of Enville Hall, pictured after restoration following a fire in 1904.

Enville Hall.

The south front and entrance.

The remarkable and ornate conservatory which housed specimen exotic plants from around the world was built in 1855 and was described as being 'second only to Crystal Palace' for sheer size and magnificence. It was demolished in 1927. Extraordinary though the Conservatory was, the Hall's gardens, lakes and much of the parkland attracted thousands of visitors each summer in the 1860s in their own right. At one time the gardens and parkland were so large that a staff of over thirty was employed to manage it. The first major work done on landscaping the area was by the poet and landscape designer, William Shenstone of The Leasowes, Halesowen, whose work was commemorated by Shenstone's Chapel on the edge of woodland. Later further landscaping was carried out, and so large was the area that a carriage road was built to enable visitors to travel through it.

The Sea Horse Pool, *c.* 1905. There were many fish ponds, ornamental lakes and fountains in the gardens, the fountains being gravity-fed from a four million gallon reservoir to which water was supplied through two steam-powered pumps.

A group of Hall staff, *c.* 1914. Standing, left to right: Walter Broughton (plumber), Charlie Howard (Hall/kitchen) Bert Lickett (chauffeur – presumably on Army leave). Seated: George Wood and Frank Bowen (chauffeurs).

Chauffeur Frank Bowen (above) with the family's Studebaker and (below) Sam Weaver, occupation unknown, with the Daimler.

Without doubt the biggest disaster to befall Enville Hall was the fire on 25 November 1904 which gutted much of the central part of the building. In this photograph, taken some twenty-four hours after the outbreak, can be seen one of two steam-powered horse-drawn pumps which had made a perilous 5 mile dash from Stourbridge through snow and on icebound roads. A graphic description of the fire and the frantic efforts of the Hall and Estate employees to save many of the buildings' treasures appeared in the *County Express*. The detailed report described the perilous cycle ride of a Hall employee made on snow and icebound roads to alert the Stourbridge Fire Brigade nearly 6 miles away. Hauling a heavy 'steamer' fire engine, the team of horses had several falls in the treacherous conditions before arriving at the Hall at 3.40 am. At 5.00 am, a second 'steamer' arrived from Stourbridge. Together with the Hall's own manual pump, which frequently froze up, the two engines pumped about 1,000 gallons of water an hour from the nearby Sea Horse Pool for nearly twenty-four hours.

While staff struggled to save valuable works of art from the stricken centre of the building, the firemen battled to keep the fire away from the ballroom and the library, which housed 'masterpieces of art and rare editions'. Once contained, the fire 'continued to burn for three days and smouldered for two weeks'. Throughout the whole episode, the Hall's fire brigade remained diligently on duty. The cause of the fire was never precisely established but was thought to have spread from a chimney fire in one of the guest bedrooms which was being prepared for a shooting and house party the following day.

Aware of the Hall's isolated position, Lord Stamford founded the Enville Hall Household Fire Brigade in the 1820s. Pictured is the same manual twelve-man pump built in 1826 which unsuccessfully tried to bring the blaze under control pending the arrival of the Stourbridge steam pumps. The old manual pump was restored by Kinver firemen.

Rebuilding work in progress on the central part of the Hall which was completely gutted. Remarkably the family's gold and silver plate which was stored in a strong room at the centre of the blaze was undamaged.

Enville Hall was also the centre of much field sport activity and had its own racecourse, the Harkaway Point-to-Point course. Standing by one of the fences are (left) John Braithwaite of Blundies Farm and (right) William Shepherd, parish church verger and sexton.

This picture, c. 1903, remains a mystery. Was it a gamekeeper's cottage? And where was it situated?

A Hunt Meet outside the Cat Inn. The date is unknown.

In 1950 Lord Cobham of Hagley Hall (seated second right) and the MCC President brought E.R.T. Holmes's XI in to play a centenary match against Enville Cricket Club. Those pictured (left to right, back row) are: Merritt, Maxwell, Chesterton, Morkell, Watts, Carr. Seated are Seller, Allen, Holmes, Cobham, Howarth. The Enville team is pictured overleaf.

The Enville team playing the E.R.T. Holmes's XI was no less than eighteen strong and the game ended in a draw. In this pre-match photograph are (left to right); front row: Shaw, Leadbetter, Bourne, Bissell, Parkes, Higginson, Hodges. Middle row: Ward-Booth (Rector of Enville), Oakley, Vaughan, Jordan, Taylor, Fletcher, Adams, Perry, Humphries, Major Vaughan. Back row: guest, C. Shaw, Bullock, Smith, H. Shaw, Fitton.

ACKNOWLEDGEMENTS

The authors gratefully acknowledge the assistance of Mr David Bills, President of Kinver Historical Society, for his unlimited patience in double-checking the numerous historical facts that emerged in the production of the text accompanying the photographs and for the use of vintage photographs from his own private collection. Acknowledgement is also made of the Historical Society's generosity in allowing access to their archives and Mrs Val Hampton for providing details of Miss Nancy Price. In return, the authors are happy to ask readers to contact the Historical Society should they have any village archive material they may wish to donate.

BRITAIN IN OLD PHOTOGRAPHS

Lincoln
Lincoln Cathedral
The Lincolnshire Coast
Liverpool
Around Llandudno
Around Lochaber
Theatrical London
Around Louth
The Lower Fal Estuary
Lowestoft
Luton
Lympne Airfield
Lytham St Annes
Maidenhead
Around Maidenhead
Around Malvern
Manchester
Manchester Road & Rail
Mansfield
Marlborough: A Second Selection
Marylebone & Paddington
Around Matlock
Melton Mowbray
Around Melksham
The Mendips
Merton & Morden
Middlesbrough
Midsomer Norton & Radstock
Around Mildenhall
Milton Keynes
Minehead
Monmouth & the River Wye
The Nadder Valley
Newark
Around Newark
Newbury
Newport, Isle of Wight
The Norfolk Broads
Norfolk at War
North Fylde
North Lambeth
North Walsham & District
Northallerton
Northampton
Around Norwich
Nottingham 1944–74
The Changing Face of Nottingham
Victorian Nottingham
Nottingham Yesterday & Today
Nuneaton
Around Oakham
Ormskirk & District
Otley & District
Oxford: The University
Oxford Yesterday & Today
Oxfordshire Railways: A Second Selection
Oxfordshire at School
Around Padstow
Pattingham & Wombourne

Penwith
Penzance & Newlyn
Around Pershore
Around Plymouth
Poole
Portsmouth
Poulton-le-Fylde
Preston
Prestwich
Pudsey
Radcliffe
RAF Chivenor
RAF Cosford
RAF Hawkinge
RAF Manston
RAF Manston: A Second Selection
RAF St Mawgan
RAF Tangmere
Ramsgate & Thanet Life
Reading
Reading: A Second Selection
Redditch & the Needle District
Redditch: A Second Selection
Richmond, Surrey
Rickmansworth
Around Ripley
The River Soar
Romney Marsh
Romney Marsh: A Second Selection
Rossendale
Around Rotherham
Rugby
Around Rugeley
Ruislip
Around Ryde
St Albans
St Andrews
Salford
Salisbury
Salisbury: A Second Selection
Salisbury: A Third Selection
Around Salisbury
Sandhurst & Crowthorne
Sandown & Shanklin
Sandwich
Scarborough
Scunthorpe
Seaton, Lyme Regis & Axminster
Around Seaton & Sidmouth
Sedgley & District
The Severn Vale
Sherwood Forest
Shrewsbury
Shrewsbury: A Second Selection
Shropshire Railways
Skegness
Around Skegness
Skipton & the Dales
Around Slough

Smethwick
Somerton & Langport
Southampton
Southend-on-Sea
Southport
Southwark
Southwell
Southwold to Aldeburgh
Stafford
Around Stafford
Staffordshire Railways
Around Staveley
Stepney
Stevenage
The History of Stilton Cheese
Stoke-on-Trent
Stoke Newington
Stonehouse to Painswick
Around Stony Stratford
Around Stony Stratford: A Second Selection
Stowmarket
Streatham
Stroud & the Five Valleys
Stroud & the Five Valleys: A Second Selection
Stroud's Golden Valley
The Stroudwater and Thames & Severn Canals
The Stroudwater and Thames & Severn Canals: A Second Selection
Suffolk at Work
Suffolk at Work: A Second Selection
The Heart of Suffolk
Sunderland
Sutton
Swansea
Swindon: A Third Selection
Swindon: A Fifth Selection
Around Tamworth
Taunton
Around Taunton
Teesdale
Teesdale: A Second Selection
Tenbury Wells
Around Tettenhall & Codshall
Tewkesbury & the Vale of Gloucester
Thame to Watlington
Around Thatcham
Around Thirsk
Thornbury to Berkeley
Tipton
Around Tonbridge
Trowbridge
Around Truro
TT Races
Tunbridge Wells

Tunbridge Wells: A Second Selection
Twickenham
Uley, Dursley & Cam
The Upper Fal
The Upper Tywi Valley
Uxbridge, Hillingdon & Cowley
The Vale of Belvoir
The Vale of Conway
Ventnor
Wakefield
Wallingford
Walsall
Waltham Abbey
Wandsworth at War
Wantage, Faringdon & the Vale Villages
Around Warwick
Weardale
Weardale: A Second Selection
Wednesbury
Wells
Welshpool
West Bromwich
West Wight
Weston-super-Mare
Around Weston-super-Mare
Weymouth & Portland
Around Wheatley
Around Whetstone
Whitchurch to Market Drayton
Around Whitstable
Wigton & the Solway Plain
Willesden
Around Wilton
Wimbledon
Around Windsor
Wingham, Addisham & Littlebourne
Wisbech
Witham & District
Witney
Around Witney
The Witney District
Wokingham
Around Woodbridge
Around Woodstock
Woolwich
Woolwich Royal Arsenal
Around Wootton Bassett, Cricklade & Purton
Worcester
Worcester in a Day
Around Worcester
Worcestershire at Work
Around Worthing
Wotton-under-Edge to Chipping Sodbury
Wymondham & Attleborough
The Yorkshire Wolds

To order any of these titles please telephone our distributor, Littlehampton Book Services on 01903 721596
For a catalogue of these and our other titles please ring Regina Schinner on 01453 731114